How To...

PLAY ROCK RHYTHM GUITAR

BY BROOKE ST. JAMES
TRANSCRIBED & EDITED BY TROY NELSON

To access video visit:
www.halleonard.com/mylibrary

Enter Code
8719-6891-7891-2443

ISBN 978-1-4950-2326-2

7777 W. BLUEMOUND RD. P.O. BOX 13819 MILWAUKEE, WI 53213

In Australia Contact:
Hal Leonard Australia Pty. Ltd.
4 Lentara Court
Cheltenham, Victoria, 3192 Australia
Email: ausadmin@halleonard.com.au

Visit Hal Leonard Online at
www.halleonard.com

CONTENTS

Brooke St. James got his start on guitar at age 9. His obsession with an old acoustic guitar sitting in the corner at his grandmother's house paid off when he was finally allowed to take the guitar home. A self-taught musician, Brooke spent endless hours listening to records and began to play along with the likes of Kiss, Aerosmith, Ted Nugent, Queen, Cheap Trick, Journey, and more. He joined his first band at the age of 16 playing with older musicians in night clubs. "It was a lot easier to be in bars underage back then!" After graduating high school, Brooke ventured out with a Florida-based rock act who toured the West Coast for a year straight, thus getting schooled in the ways of the road at age 17.

"From that point, I played with a few regional cover bands that really helped broaden my playing. It was funk, rock, blues, pop, reggae, you name it."

In the mid-'80s, Brooke relocated to Milwaukee where he joined forces with Moxy Roxx. Moxy was filling large venues, which garnered the attention of Cheap Trick manager Ken Adamany. Moxy released one studio album, *Victims of the Night*, which grew to cult status and grabbed the attention of a few major labels. Unfortunately, a half-hearted effort by management killed any potential for a deal and major-label interest soon fizzled.

After struggling for five years with Moxy, Brooke felt that if anything was going to happen, he would need to get to Los Angeles or New York City. After some contacts were made, it was off to New York to form what would become Tyketto, a hard rock group that was eventually signed to Geffen Records. Brooke wrote and recorded four studio albums and did numerous world tours before leaving the band officially in 2014.

Brooke did a three-year stint in Las Vegas with classic rock act Yellow Brick Road. As of 2016, Brooke is currently playing with the bands Rhythm Method, Light Up (A Tribute to Styx), and the Yuletide Conspiracy Project, as well as doing session work and writing songs for a forthcoming solo album.

INTRODUCTION

 **INTRODUCTION**

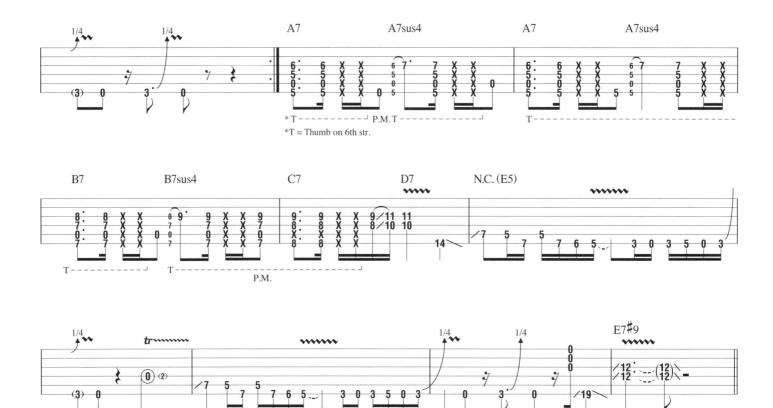

Hello, my name is Brooke St. James and I want to share some of what I consider to be the fundamentals of playing good, solid rock 'n' roll rhythm guitar. Since I'm an ear-trained player, we won't get into all the confusing theory stuff; we'll just stick to the basics. After all, it's just rock 'n' roll, right? OK, let's get started…

ABOUT THE VIDEO

Each chapter in the book includes a full video lesson, so you can see and hear the material being taught. To access all of the videos that accompany this book, simply go to **www.halleonard.com/ mylibrary** and enter the code found on page 1. The music examples that include video are marked with an icon throughout the book, and the timecode listed with each icon tells you exactly where on the video the example is performed.

CHAPTER 1
STRUMMING

In this first segment, I'd like to talk to you about strumming. If you've played any guitar at all, and I'm assuming you have, you're probably familiar with open-chord strumming like the example below.

▶ STRUMMING 1 - 0:25

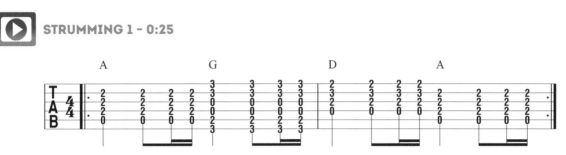

This type of rhythm playing works best with a clean tone. As we move into the rock genre and start adding gain or distortion, you can see where you might start to get into trouble. If this is the intro to a song, it might be OK. But when the band's playing, this type of rhythm playing can get really crowded, really quickly.

THE DOWNSTROKE

When using what I like to call the "powerstroke," or *downstroke*, one of the first things I do is use a barre chord in place of an open chord—in this case, A. It gives you a tighter punch and allows you to control the rhythm a little bit better.

The downstroke is about adding a pulse, or bounce, to the rhythm. It adds a punch that helps the drums and bass drive the rhythm of the song. Notice that I'm using palm muting (indicated by "P.M." in the notation). You'll learn more about this in Chapter 2.

▶ STRUMMING 2 - 1:42

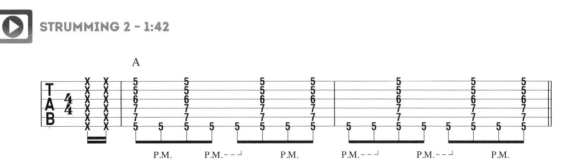

THE UPSTROKE

The opposite of the downstroke is the *upstroke*. These two concepts work in tandem.

▶ STRUMMING 3 - 2:00

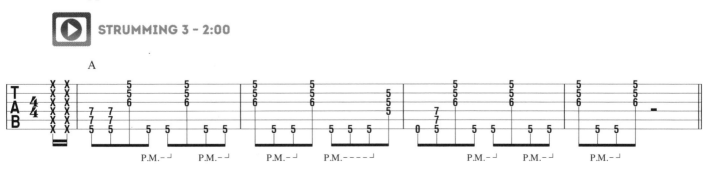

In this next example, I'm simply alternating downstrokes and upstrokes. There's really no set pattern; sometimes you can pop those high strings with a downstroke, and sometimes it's best to hit them with an upstroke. The key is to keep your right hand moving back and forth.

STRUMMING 4 - 2:20

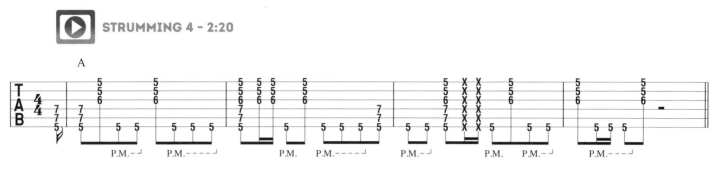

As you can see, I never stop driving the right hand. Otherwise, it's very difficult to keep your timing together. I also recommend tapping your toe to help you keep the feel of the music steady and in time.

PEDAL TONES

The next topic I want to discuss is *pedal tones*. As far as rock 'n' roll is concerned, most guitarists start on the low E string. You can incorporate any string, but the low E is a good place to begin.

STRUMMING 5 - 3:03

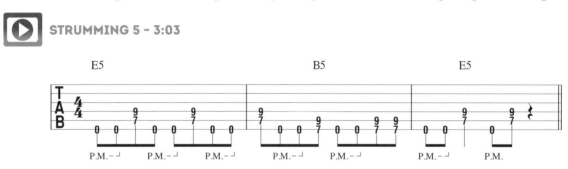

The premise of the pedal tone is that you're moving between different chords or voicings while using a central chord or note to anchor the movement. Here, I'm using the low E string to anchor an E5–C5–D5 progression.

STRUMMING 6 - 3:29

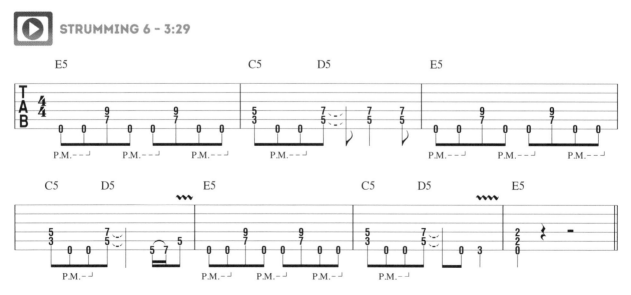

You can use pedal tones in a number of different ways—there are no particular rules—but I like to use the low E as a starting spot because it's a nice, powerful-sounding open string and it's very rock 'n' roll. Same goes for the open A string, as in this next example. We were using eighth notes in the previous examples, but we can also incorporate 16th notes. Notice the wavy line above the G5 chords in this example. This slight shaking of the strings is called *vibrato*. You'll learn more about it in Chapter 5.

STRUMMING 7 – 4:10

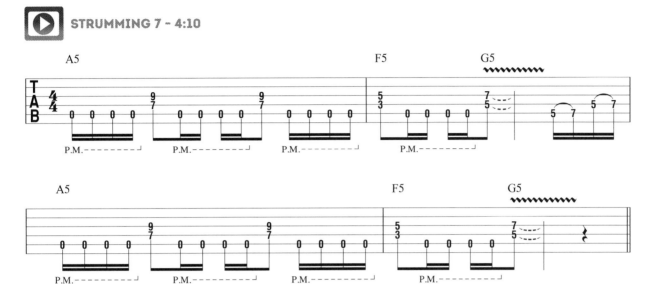

Sixteenth notes really drive the band, although they do have a metallic edge to them in this context. The thing to remember is: there are no rules. In fact, you could *swing* the 16th notes.

STRUMMING 8 – 4:38

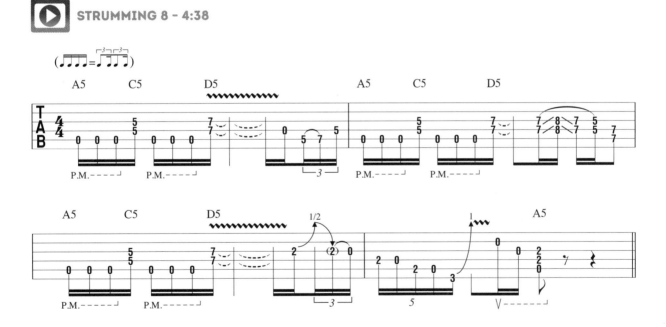

Pedal tones will work pretty much any way you use them; it's all about having those alternating pedal tones driving what you're doing around them.

In this chapter's final example, I'm going to show you what to do—and what not to do—when you're playing some of these rhythm parts. You'll notice that, as I play along with the drums, the first half of the progression is a little crowded and "loosey-goosey." Meanwhile, the second half of the progression starts to tighten up right away. The main takeaway here is that I'm playing to the bass drum, the snare drum, and the hi-hat, thereby pulling the rhythm together and creating space for the other instruments. This helps to drive the rhythm forward.

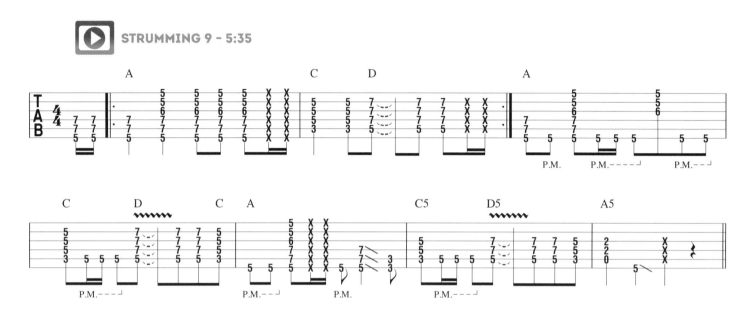

STRUMMING 9 - 5:35

CHAPTER 2
MUTING

It's very important to have muting nailed down if you want to play rock rhythm guitar. It gives you the percussive element that you'll need to get that "drum factor" in your rhythm playing.

I'm going to start by talking about the edge of the palm, which you'll be using to *palm mute*. I've already played some examples that use palm muting in Chapter 1. You want to lay the edge of the palm across the strings and "bounce" it as the rhythm dictates.

Here's an example that uses no palm muting:

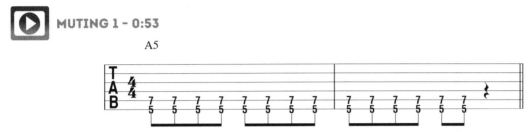

Now here's an example that incorporates palm muting:

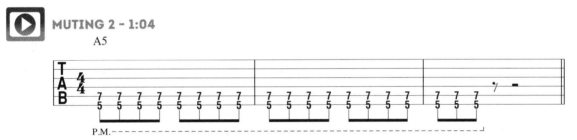

The bounce should be apparent in this example. It's achieved by laying the right-hand palm across the strings.

Here's another example that utilizes palm muting:

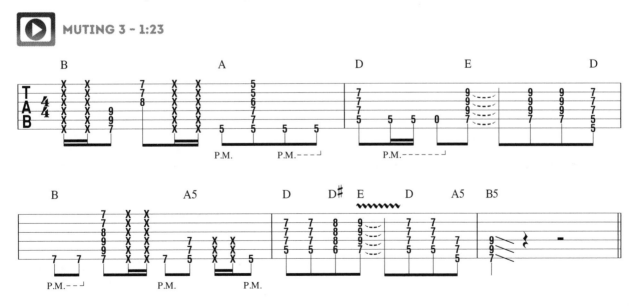

When you bring the right-hand muting in and out of the example, it really makes all of the notes "pop" and the chords jump and separate. It also makes room for the rest of the instruments in the band.

PULSE MUTING

Another thing that goes along with palm muting is something that I like to call "pulse muting." It's essentially the incorporation of your left hand. The following example incorporates both left- and right-hand muting.

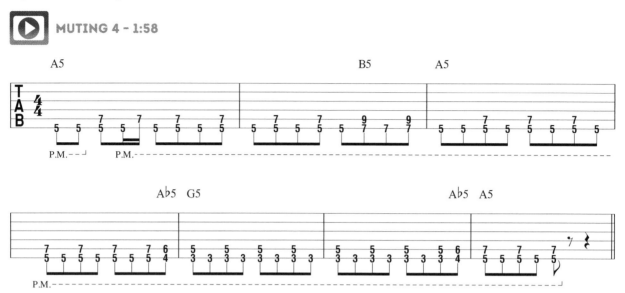

MUTING 4 - 1:58

In that example, my left hand is bouncing a bit. It's a real physical thing: I'm squeezing the strings as I accent the chords, then releasing pressure so as to only mute the sixth string between chord attacks, which causes the strings to "pulse." I could try to get that choo-choo train chug exclusively with my right hand, but it doesn't come across unless you're able to get those notes to stop and start again. Pulse muting is very effective and lends itself to driving a band.

Here's an example that everything we've learned so far together. It should help you pick up the right- and left-hand muting vibe a little bit more.

MUTING 5 - 3:47

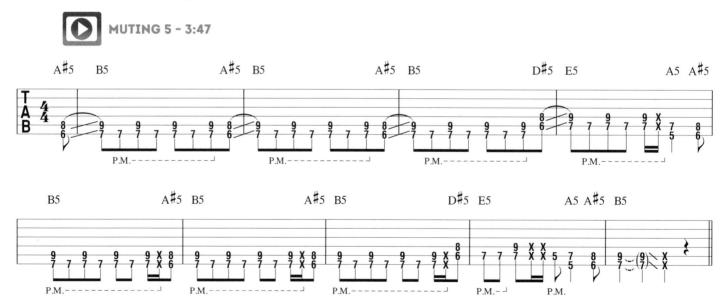

Keep in mind that, as you start to explore these muting techniques, the concept itself is pretty easy to grasp, but it takes years to perfect. Therefore, I recommend that you start slowly. If you attack it at 1,000 miles per hour, it'll lead to frustration. What you're after is the *feel*. You want to make sure that you have the correct feel and that both hands are doing their jobs to get that pulse going.

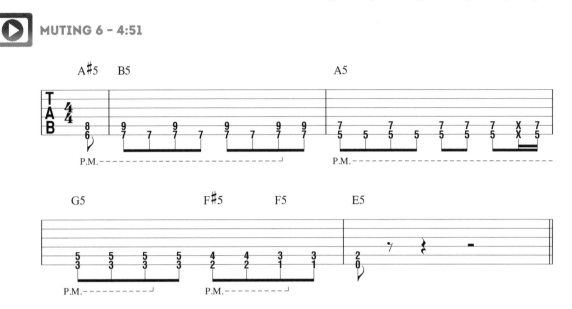

MUTING 6 - 4:51

Here's an example that incorporates alternate strumming (upstrokes and downstrokes) and left- and right-hand muting to create some dynamic rhythm playing.

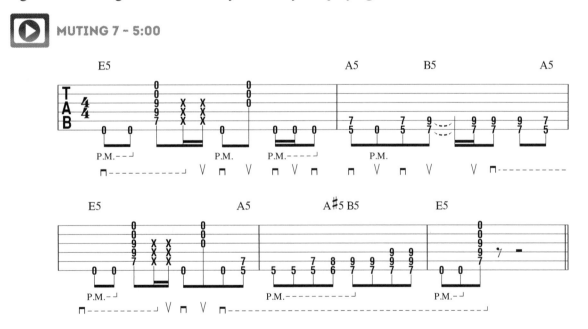

MUTING 7 - 5:00

CHAPTER 3

BARRE CHORDS AND POWER CHORDS

In this chapter, I want to talk to you about barre chords and power chords. We're going to break them down and talk about different places on the neck where you can play these chords, plus how to best use them to make your songs sound cool.

E-SHAPE BARRE CHORD

Let's start with a basic E-shape barre chord.

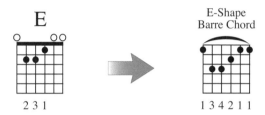

What we're doing is taking a basic open-position E major chord and moving it up the neck. Your left-hand index finger now becomes the nut, replacing the open strings of the E major chord. If we play this shape at the fifth fret, we get an A major chord, and so on.

A-SHAPE BARRE CHORD

You can do the same thing with the open-position A major chord:

D-SHAPE BARRE CHORD

You can do the same thing with the open-position D major chord, although the note on the high E string is typically omitted, making this shape a "power chord" because the chord's 3rd (in this case, F♯) is not played. This leaves only the root (D) and 5th (A), the two notes that comprise a power chord.

In summary, the root of the E shape is located on the sixth string, the root of the A shape is located on the fifth string, and the root of the D shape is located on the fourth string.

You can play the open A chord all day long and get some great power-chord riffs, but if you want to play something that really cuts through the instrumentation around you, something like the following might be a better choice.

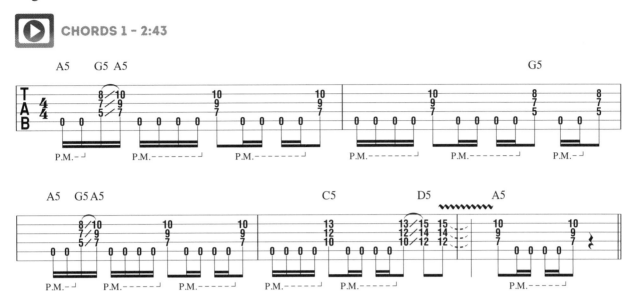

CHORDS 1 - 2:43

Now you're an octave higher, making room for the instruments around you. Not everything you play has to be based on the E-shape barre chord; sometimes an E chord might sound better when played as an A-shape or D-shape barre chord (or power chord). These shapes open up other possibilities.

THE BOOGIE PATTERN

This next example is a classic rock 'n' roll move. You don't hear it quite as much anymore, but it's really a staple in rock 'n' roll rhythm guitar playing. I call it the "pinky pedal tone," but you might hear others call it a "blues shuffle" or "boogie pattern." We start with the B power chord at the seventh fret, but instead of walking chords around a single bass note, we're going to walk two single notes around one chord. This one requires palm muting and a pinky stretch up to the 11th fret of the A string. It adds nice motion to the chord and progression. You could sit and play it for five minutes and not get tired of it.

CHORDS 2 - 4:40

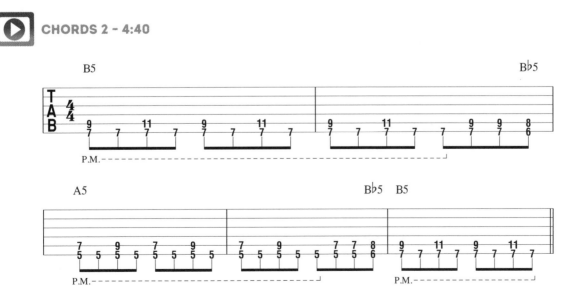

Once you start to feel really confident with this figure, you can move the pinky all the way up to the 12th fret:

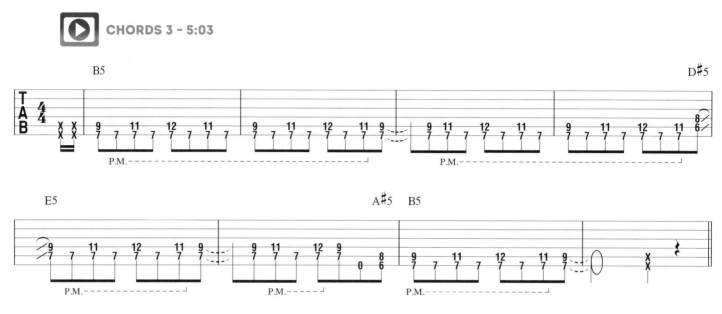

Even if you don't use this type of rhythm in your own songs, you should be aware of it because it's such a staple of rock 'n' roll rhythm guitar playing.

G-SHAPE BARRE CHORD

Before we go any further, I should also point out that it's possible to play power chords based on the G string, as well.

Although not as common as some of the other shapes, the G-shape power chord is effective as a "color" chord.

5THS

Next, I'd like to talk about subdividing barre chords; that is, tightening up the voicings a bit. You've probably noticed that more experienced guitarists tend to move away from playing the full, six-string barre chords. There are two reasons for this: 1) they're cumbersome when moving quickly around the neck, and 2) the top (higher) notes can sometimes get in the way of other instruments.

So what you'll see is a lot of rhythm guitar players limiting their voicings to two or three notes. As I mentioned earlier, if you play just the chord's root and 5th (fifth note of its relative major scale), you get a power chord. If you play the E-shape barre chord at the fifth fret, you get an A major chord. If you eliminate the top strings, playing only strings 6–4, you get an A power chord (notated as "A5"). The top strings, low to high, contain the 3rd (in this case, C♯) and repetitions of the 5th (E) and root (A).

Sometimes you want your chords to sit tightly in the arrangement, and power chords are much easier to navigate than their six-string relatives—and much easier to play in a tighter, focused fashion. It's important that the chords fit with the other instruments around them, especially in a band with two guitarists playing with a distorted tone.

4THS

Now I'd like to discuss 4ths. For these next two examples, I'm using my fingers to pick the strings. Learn more about this technique in Chapter 5.

CHORDS 4 - 8:26

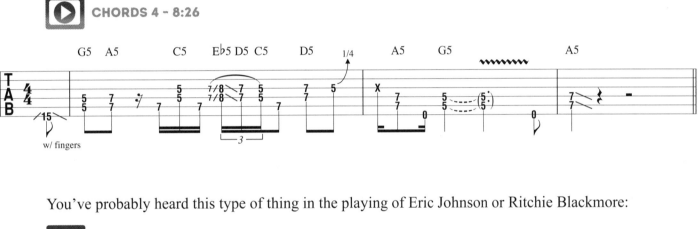

You've probably heard this type of thing in the playing of Eric Johnson or Ritchie Blackmore:

CHORDS 5 - 8:39

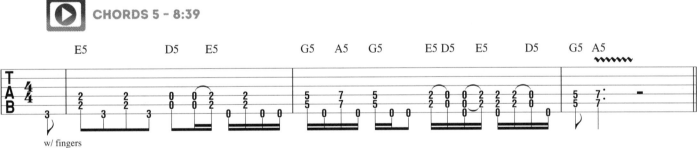

What they're doing is taking the 5th, or power chord, and placing the root note on top rather than in the chord's bass. We're leaving the lower root out and instead playing the 5th in the bass. It changes the timbre of the chord because the notes are stacked differently—the interval is a 4th rather than a 5th. Fourths are really effective and sometimes sound bigger than a full, six-string barre-chord voicing.

Every rock guitar player that's ever walked the face of the earth has used these intervals at some point. You'll hear them time and time again, and, at some point, you'll use them in your music, too.

In this chapter, we're going to talk about something that I like to call "melodic rhythm." It's really nothing more than taking your basic chords and moving some of the voicings around.

USING THE G-SHAPE POWER CHORD

In the first example, we're going to use the G-shape power chord with the 5th (D) in the bass:

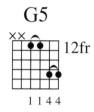

By barring the D, G, and B strings with the index finger, the other fingers are free to move around:

 MELODIC RHYTHM 1 - 0:31

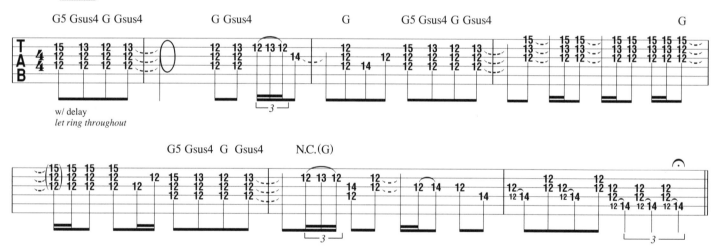

Against a great rhythm track, that type of figure can add a really nice dimension.

USING OPEN STRINGS

You'll see guitarists like U2's the Edge play this sort of stuff. He'll also incorporate open strings, like this:

 MELODIC RHYTHM 2 - 1:41

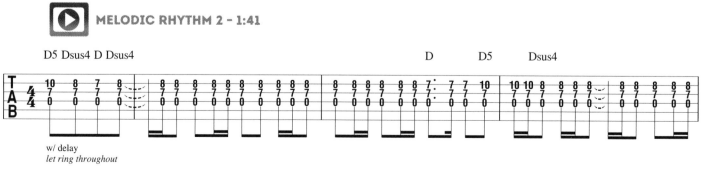

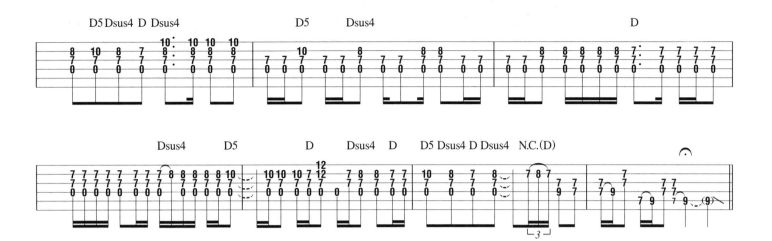

USING OPEN AND MUTED STRINGS

Here's another example that uses not only open strings, but some muted strings as well. It starts with the B barre-chord shape at the seventh fret and incorporates some open strings—mainly the E and B strings on top—along with some alternating 3rds and 4ths. I'm muting the A string—it's not being voiced. The bass note is then moved to the C♯ note at the ninth fret of string 6 and then to the open A string before returning to the B note at fret 7.

▶ MELODIC RHYTHM 3 - 3:30

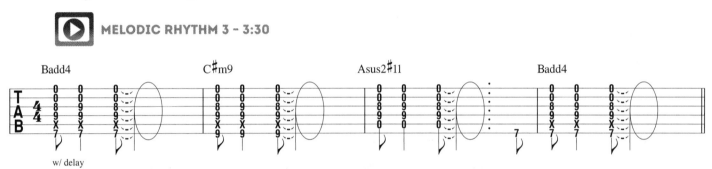

The goal is to find some great "moving" tones to play in conjunction with open strings, while muting unwanted tones so only the complimentary notes ring out.

USING MOVING CHORDS

I want to show you something else that I use a lot. In fact, a lot of rock guitar players use it. It's very utilitarian and cool and can be used in so many ways. By simply taking the power-chord shape and moving one finger down a *half step* (one fret), up a half step, or up a *whole step* (two frets), a lot of cool stuff starts to happen. Check this out:

▶ MELODIC RHYTHM 4 - 4:23

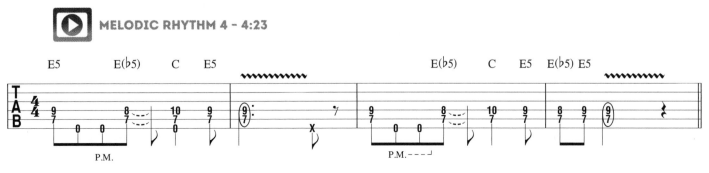

All that I'm doing is taking that good ol' E power chord with the 5th (B) on top and moving it up and down the fourth string in half steps and whole steps. Each increment has a new surprise. You just have to play around with it and you'll get some cool sounds, as in the example below.

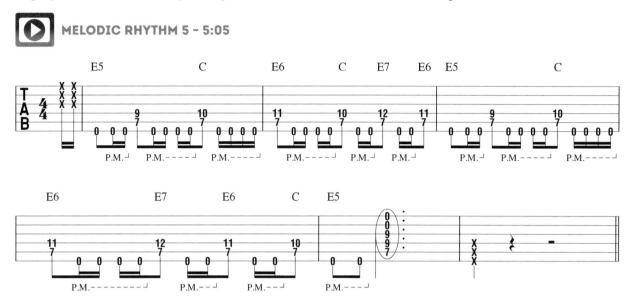

MELODIC RHYTHM 5 - 5:05

PLAYING IN A MAJOR KEY

You can also get some really nice effects using a major key:

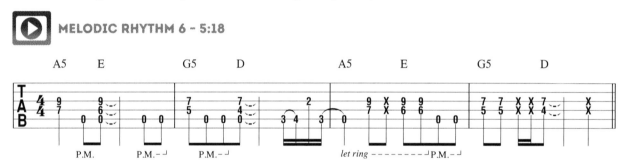

MELODIC RHYTHM 6 - 5:18

That figure is just crying for a great melody. These are great writing tools and things to experiment with when you're looking for different voicings. If you're playing with another guitar player and looking for something that sounds really cool, this is a great place to experiment, so give it a shot!

CHAPTER 5
CHORD-BASED RIFFS

▶ CHORD RIFFS 1 - 0:00

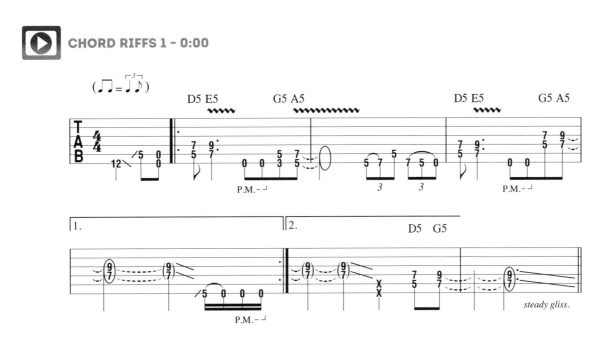

In this chapter, I'm going to give you a couple of examples and then break them down to show you how they work together really nicely. The first one goes like this:

▶ CHORD RIFFS 2 - 0:25

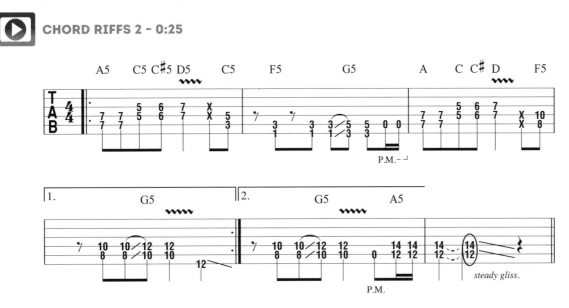

That figure contains a fast-moving riff. I'm barring the A and D strings at the seventh fret with my ring finger, the D and G strings at the fifth fret with my index finger, and then walking it up. Next, I slide down the neck to play syncopated power chords, shifting from C5 at the third fret to F5 at the first fret and, finally, the G5 at the third fret. The last move is simply F5 to G5 in the upper register. I like the way this figure finishes in the upper octave, because sometimes when you finish in the lower octave, it doesn't come across as impactful. Plus, we've already spent time in the lower octave. It's a nice period at the end of the sentence.

Here's another riff for you. Once again, we use those beautiful 4ths!

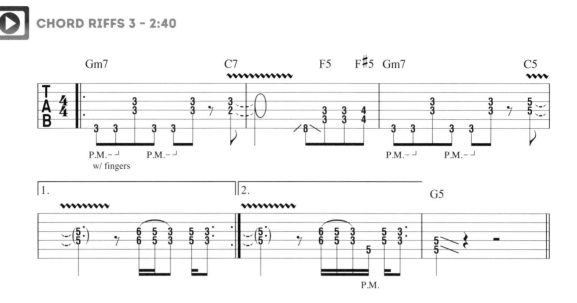

CHORD RIFFS 3 - 2:40

Basically, what I'm doing here is *hybrid picking*. You can use either your thumb or a guitar pick in conjunction with your other fingers. You'll get a softer sound with your thumb. I use my thumb because I want the sixth string to pop and snap a bit. It's just a matter of taste; there's no real rule to it.

Start with your middle finger on the G note at the third fret of the low E string and your ring finger and pinky on the third fret of the D and G strings, respectively. You're playing the F note with your ring finger, and what you're going to do is move down a half step to the E note on the second fret, which is played with the index finger. This allows you to leave the G bass note in place. It creates a pretty dramatic effect.

Next, we're walking up in 4ths again and then quickly sliding back to the opening riff. The 4ths act as a brief interruption but still keep the figure rolling. The final portion of the figure involves some quick movement. I'm using my ring finger, middle finger, and index finger, starting on the sixth fret with the ring finger, which pulls off to the middle finger (fret 5) and then the index finger (fret 3). These quick 4ths then send us back to the top of the riff again.

This is a pretty cool, simple riff, but one thing that I think adds even more drama to it is *chord vibrato*. I like to shake the strings at various distances to give it a "chorusing" effect. It gives the chord some swagger. Chord vibrato will add a lot of snap to your playing and is something that you'll want to work on. You should try it at different places on the neck. You'll hear this type of vibrato in the playing of Gary Moore and John Sykes, among others. It's something that you'll definitely want to incorporate into your rhythm guitar playing.

Here's another example that incorporates chord vibrato:

CHORD RIFFS 4 - 7:12

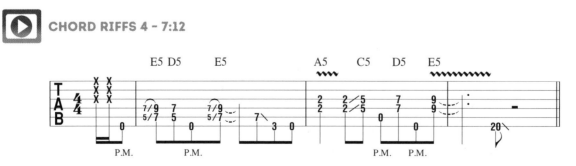

CHAPTER 6
NOTE-BASED RIFFS

▶ NOTE RIFFS 1 - 0:00

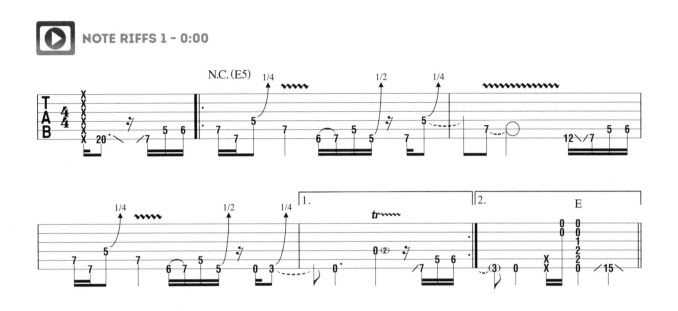

In this chapter, we're going to discuss building single-note riffs. I love bands that use linear lines that the bass and guitar play together. You find this type of playing in Whitesnake, Led Zeppelin, etc. Note-based riffs are a really easy way to add a super-cool hook and motion to your song. The riff above would be virtually impossible to play with chords.

Let's talk about what's going on in this riff and what makes it so cool. First of all, it's very bluesy and pentatonic-based, with a lot of passing tones. Sometimes those nasty chromatic pitches just sound great together! I'm starting with my ring finger on the seventh fret of the low E string and then walking chromatically up the A string with my index, middle, and ring fingers. This is where it starts to get tricky: I'm rolling back down to the B note on string 6 with my ring finger. You'll want to work on getting that smooth. Next, we skip a string, jumping up to the D string for a quarter-step bend before landing on the seventh fret of the A string with the ring finger.

The next part of the riff starts with a hammer-on from the sixth to seventh fret of the low E string, which is followed by the index finger on the fifth fret of the A string. The index finger is then rolled back down to the low E string for a half-step bend. In my opinion, this is the coolest part of the riff. In the first part of the riff, I go high for the quarter-step bend, and then low for the second part. This gives a call-and-response aspect to the riff—it's a question with an answer.

This next example is somewhat similar to the previous one, but it has a couple of different aspects.

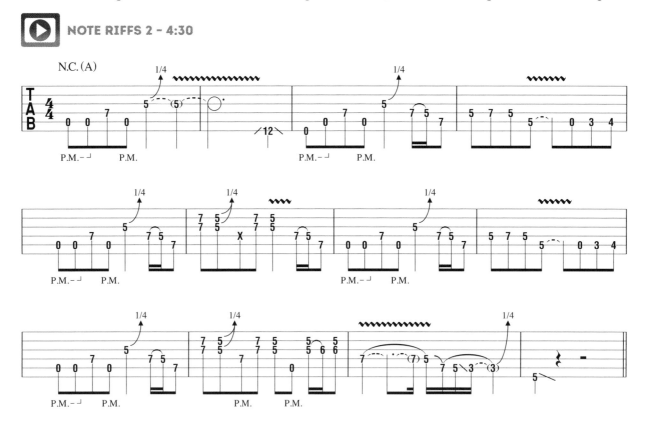

Although I'm not using chords, it's the same premise: I'm pedaling an eighth-note pattern and moving to different notes. I'm just playing a pretty simple blues pattern, but it's not just that; it's also the rhythm and the space in between the notes that gives it a sexier vibe. My favorite part of any riff like this is that you've got an opportunity with some space to put a little English on a couple of the notes. It gives them a push/pull tension.

GLISSANDO

In addition to the ideas we've already discussed, *glissando*, or "gliss," can be really effective. If there's nothing else happening in a certain spot in the music, a gliss (slide) can be really cool. Ted Nugent made a career out of 'em! Here's an example:

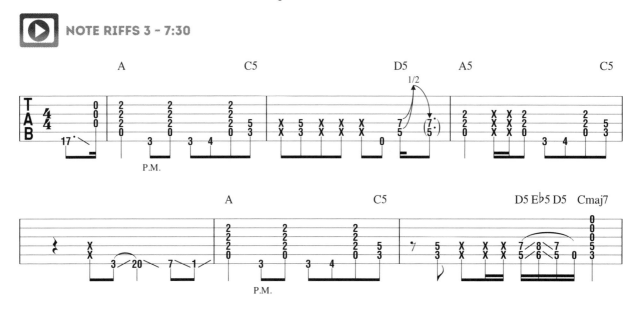

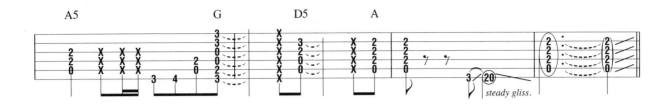

Glissando technique is really powerful, especially if you have a spot where you can do it in unison with your bass player (Van Halen has songs that start that way).

TREMOLO-PICKED GLISS

The *tremolo-picked gliss* is a similar technique that you can incorporate into your playing.

 NOTE RIFFS 4 - 8:08

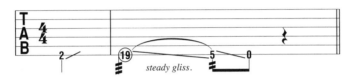

While you're sliding down the sixth string, pick it in a 16th-note rhythm. You can play it in time or you can play it out of time—either is fine. It can be done on any string, anywhere. The bottom line: it adds attitude.

CHORD SCRATCHING

Tremolo picking, scratching, sliding… these are all things you hear but don't really think about. Here's an example that incorporates chord scratching:

 NOTE RIFFS 5 - 8:48

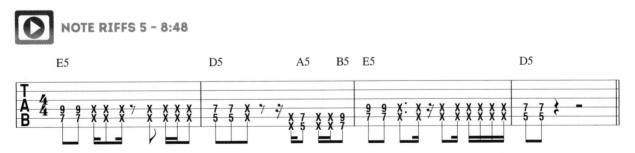

Used sparingly, these are great effects. You might want to try them in your own playing.

CHAPTER 7
CHORD VOICINGS AND THE "BIG PICTURE"

When I'm putting together my own riffs or songs, I try to envision the music that I'm creating as a painting. All of the notes and chords collectively create a canvas. I imagine the whole sound spectrum: guitars, drums, bass, horns, keyboards, etc. As guitar players, a lot of times, the ideas we think are going to sound awesome don't always sound awesome in that painting. You have to make room for all of the other elements in the painting, too. Otherwise, you end up painting everything with one color.

For example, if you had this type of progression…

▶ VOICINGS 1 - 0:53

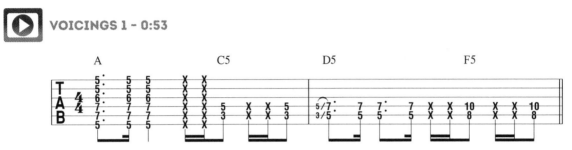

…and played it like that all the way through the song, nothing's going to breathe; you're going to have a one-dimensional painting. What I'm hoping to show you in this next example are some ways of painting that picture with different voicings of the same chords so you make room for the things that also need to be a part of that painting.

For example, if we had a part that goes like this…

▶ VOICINGS 2 - 1:33

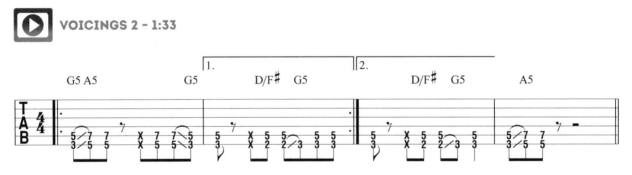

…it sounds fine by itself. Perhaps you could start the song with that (there's a myriad of ways to approach it). The problem is, when everything else comes in—the drums, bass, vocals, etc.—they're all competing for sonic space. It's like you have a family of six and everyone wants to ride in the front! It just doesn't work, so you have to make some room.

Here's one way to approach it:

▶ VOICINGS 3 - 2:19

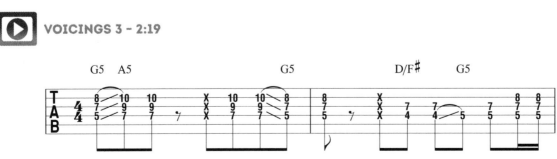

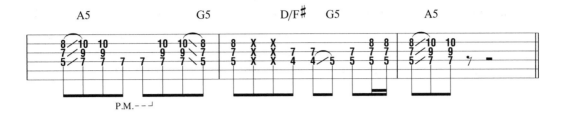

By using that brighter, higher-octave voicing, you can see how everything around it is going to breathe much easier. You could even take it a step further and move it all the way up to the 12th fret:

▶ **VOICINGS 4 - 2:50**

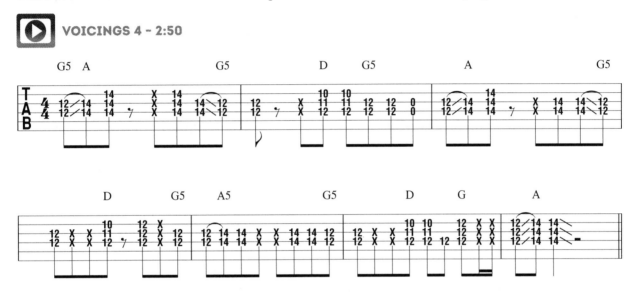

By experimenting with different voicings and different places on the neck, you're going to find the right one for the right moments in the song. You don't have to be a "theory guy" or "music guru" to have an ear to find what sounds good. But you do need to play along with other people and listen. So experiment with these different voicings, different positions, and different registers and see what works for you!

Let's expand on the idea of finding great voicings that work in your musical application, whether it's on a recording or playing in a band. The following is a personal example. I had a simple progression that I wanted to use, Em–D–A, and I wanted it to be a driving rhythm within the song structure, like this:

▶ **VOICINGS 5 - 4:05**

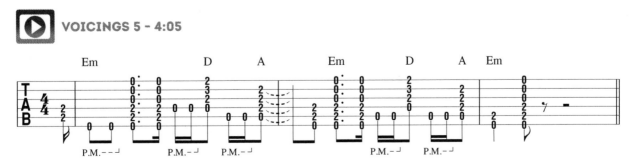

I needed it to sound big, powerful, nasty, and rock 'n' roll. Unfortunately, those voicings weren't too pleasant or interesting, so I started experimenting. I got away from the deep, dark Em voicing that I was using and moved it up to seventh position. Right away it helped me—it popped right out. While the open-position D chord sounded beefy, it was incongruent with the new Em voicing—I needed something that sounded like the chords lived together nicely, so I moved my D chord to the seventh fret. The last chord in the equation was A. I decided to place it up the neck with the other voicings, playing a seventh-position power chord on strings 4–2.

VOICINGS 6 - 5:26

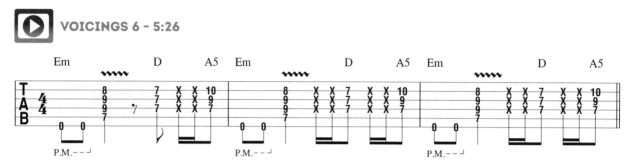

Then I started playing around with these new voicings to see if I could come up with something even more interesting. What happened was I stumbled upon an A major voicing with the 3rd, C#, in the bass. I loved it because it widened the sound and enhanced the melody while still getting the job done.

VOICINGS 7 - 6:01

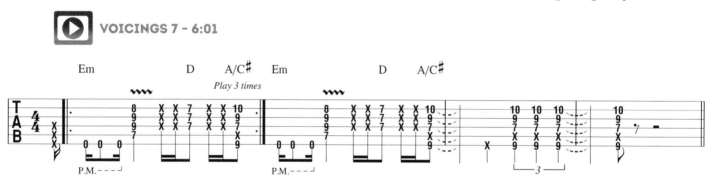

Compared to the open voicings, it was a no-brainer. It worked really well. If you use this idea in your music, you'll find some amazing things. Don't just go with the first thing that occurs to you; look a little deeper and you'll find some great stuff.

CHAPTER 8
COMBINED RIFFS

 COMBINED RIFFS 1 - 0:00

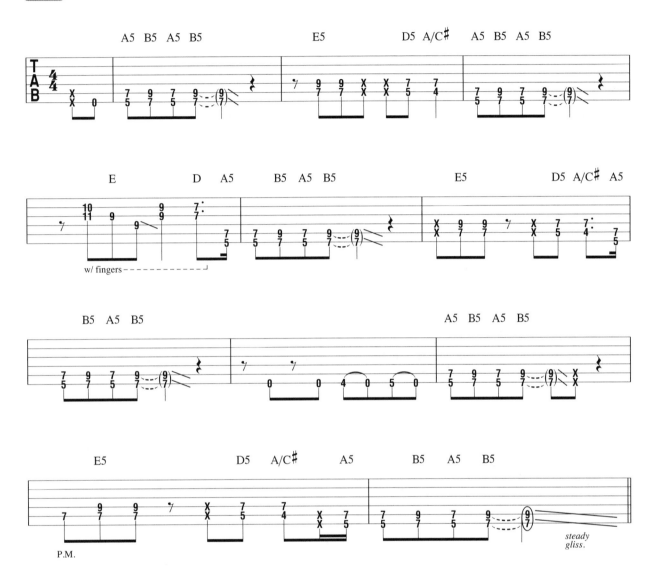

The example above is a combination of some of the chords we've already covered, as well as hybrid picking, moving voicings, and single-note lines. If you put all of those ingredients together in the pot—single notes, power chords, moving voicings, and hybrid picking—it gets really interesting to listen to; you get a lot of variations to draw from. One of my favorite bands of all time, AC/DC, has built a career from this type of playing—living proof that it's something that works really well.

Here's another example of combined riffing. All of the techniques that we've previously discussed come together for some really interesting-sounding stuff. Whereas I opened with chords in this chapter's first example, this time I lead with single notes before finishing with some hybrid picking to give the figure some snotty attitude.

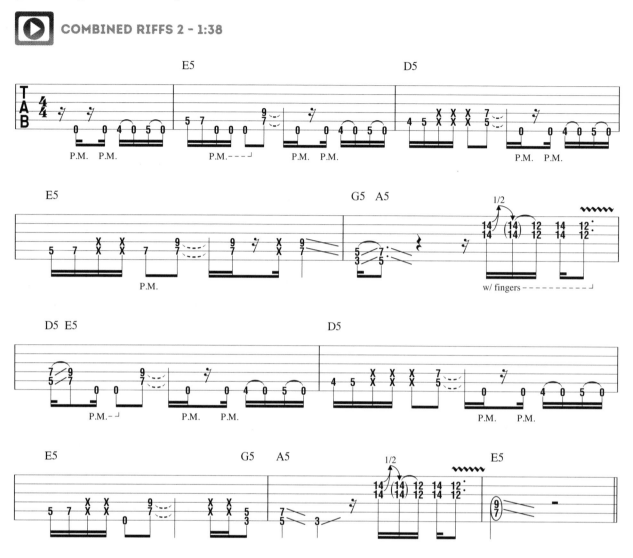

COMBINED RIFFS 2 - 1:38

ADDING SPACE

Something that we haven't touched on too much is the importance of space in your riffs. AC/DC are the masters of this; they knew exactly where to put the empty spots for the snare drum to come down or the vocal to come through. They own that technique. Because of it, they're one of the most copied bands today. Next up is an example that uses some space. The wavy arrow preceding the first and last notes means to upstrum the strings a little slower than usual (from highest to lowest string).

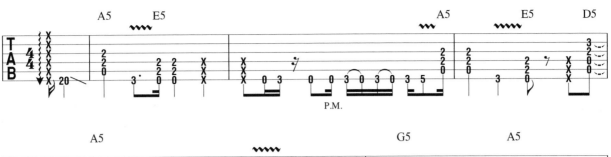

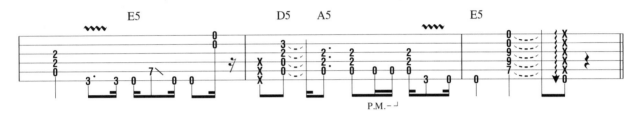

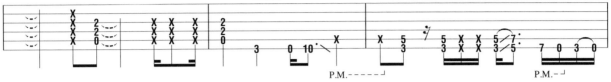

The following is another riff that is inspired by AC/DC. Hopefully, the spaces that I interject will help you understand why the technique is so cool.

COMBINED RIFFS 4 - 3:46

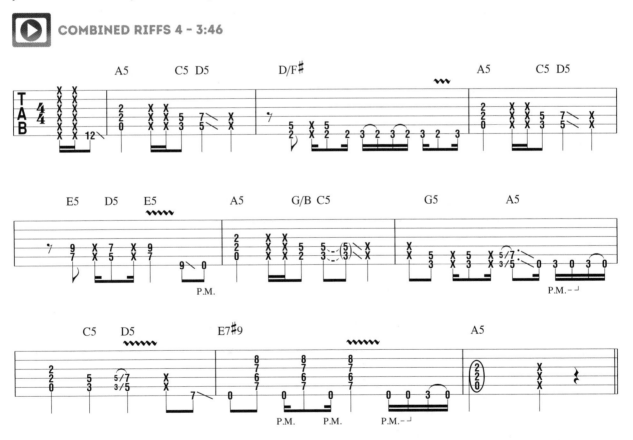

The figure above should help get the idea across—that is, the spaces between the notes and chords are essentially what give the riff its power. If your riff doesn't breathe, it tends to get kind of boring and rundown very quickly.

Here's an example that incorporates a drumbeat (see video). It contains power chords, space, riffs, and single notes, all of which will show you the power of including space between the notes and chords.

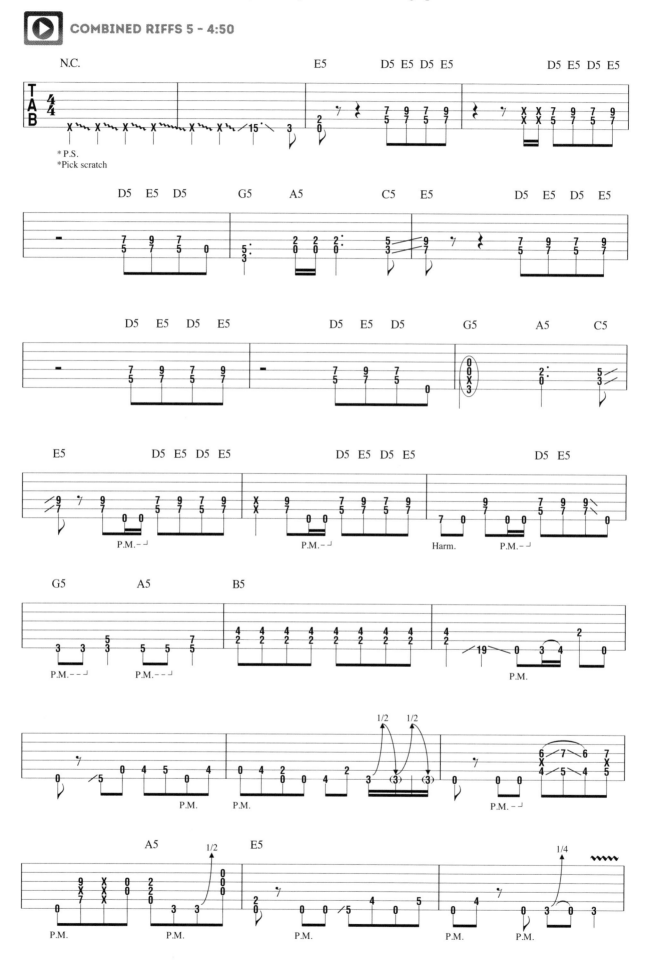

COMBINED RIFFS 5 - 4:50

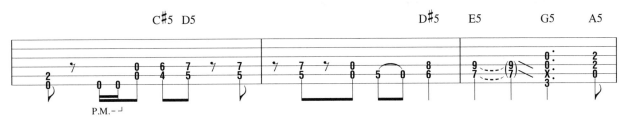

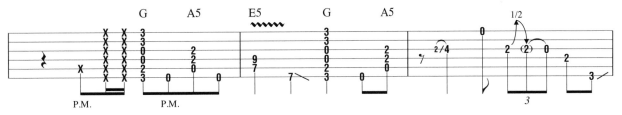

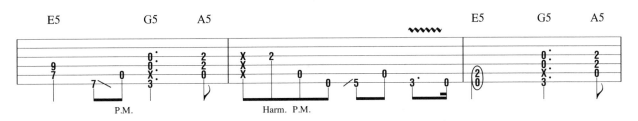

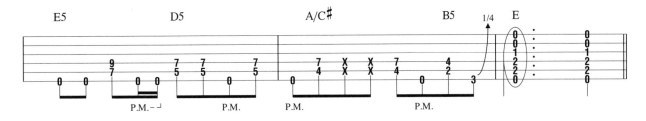

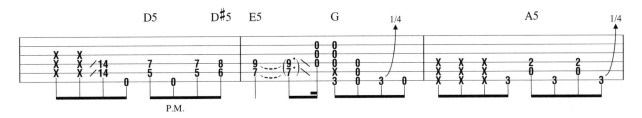

CHAPTER 9
CREATING YOUR OWN RIFFS

▶ **CREATING RIFFS 1 - 0:00**

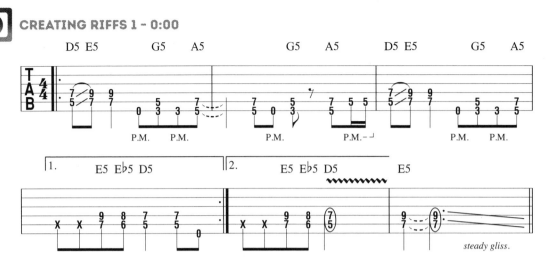

The riff above is a really simple example of using moving chords, but what I really want to point out is that there's nothing particularly special about the progression—it's neither bad nor good; it's just a bunch of chords put together. What makes it special is the way in which you approach it. The three things you really need to think about are: 1) playing with good timing, 2) having the right attitude and approach, and 3) the attack. You need to make the music your own when you pick up the guitar and lay something down. It can't be "namby-pamby"—you've got to hit it!

Here's the same idea played differently:

▶ **CREATING RIFFS 2 - 1:52**

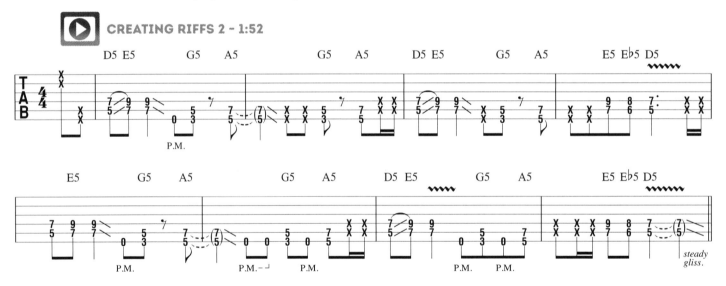

The chords are the same, but the difference is the timing, attitude, and attack, which can breathe new life into an even average guitar riff. Another thing: it's very important to tap your foot and really feel the music when you play. That will help you achieve the proper attitude. When your body is moving, it's hard not to get into the music.

▶ **CREATING RIFFS 3 - 2:10**

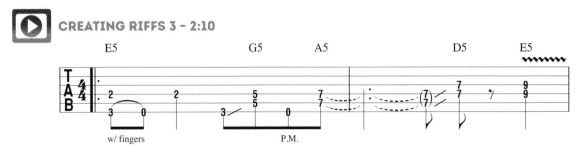

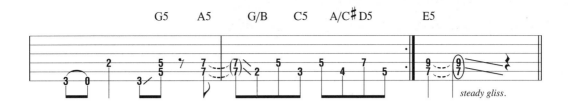

You might've noticed that the example above is similar to the first riff that I played in this chapter; I just approached it from a different angle. Something that I often do is record what I'm playing and, as I get a riff idea, I keep developing it. It may turn into three, four, or five different riffs before I'm done. It's a great way to practice. In fact, if you add a click or drum loop, it's really going to help you develop as a player while you create.

The riff opens with a fingerpicked pull-off and then moves to a couple of sets of 4ths. The pull-off figure reappears in measure 3, followed by the first set of 4ths and a walking pattern (I'm walking up the neck like a spider and landing on the D note on fret 5 of the A string). Shaking those strings doesn't hurt either; it gives the riff a little attitude.

RECORD YOURSELF

▶ CREATING RIFFS 4 - 4:46

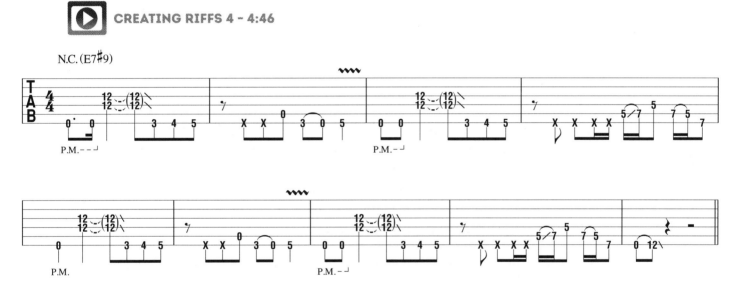

That was another variation on the original idea. Again, I suggest that you record yourself when you're creating. It really helps with your timing and intensity. Listen to the way you're hitting your instrument, the way you're attacking the strings, and your attitude—all of that. You might think you remember what you played, but it might not be exactly right. However, if you record it, it is what it is—you'll have an exact recall of the notes, attitude, attack, and intensity.

You may have noticed the drum fill that opened the previous example. It had a big downbeat and you may have been anticipating a big guitar to enter, but that didn't happen. Instead, I decided to leave some space on beat 1. As a result, it leaves room for something else, perhaps a horn stab to create a call-and-answer phrase. You may have also noticed that I've added some rhythm guitar color—palm mutes, vibrato, etc. That type of stuff goes a long way. Try to incorporate these techniques when you're creating your own riffs. And remember: record, record, record!

CHAPTER 10
UNDERSTANDING "FEEL"

In this chapter, I want to talk to you about "feel." Growing up, I was listening to bands like Led Zeppelin, the Rolling Stones, Aerosmith, and Van Halen. All of these rock 'n' roll bands incorporated a lot of different feels into their music. As my rhythm playing developed, I started to realize that there was something interesting going on: there were times when the music sounded really urgent, and there were other times when the music felt like it slowed down. There were a number of different feels that came through that music that I learned to develop, but it wasn't until later that I started to put a name to those things.

PUSH FEEL

I want to run through a couple of examples and then talk about what they are and why they do what they do to music.

 **FEEL 1 - 0:52**

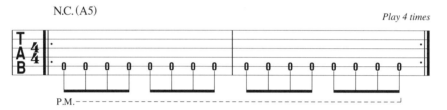

What I did there was just pedal along on the open A string to a kick and snare beat (see video). I'm trying to show you there is a "push" feel, or sense of urgency. The guitar rhythm I am playing is in front of the beat. If you could look at it on a graph, you would see that my pick is literally striking the string before the drums are hitting. That's going to give you a pushed, or urgent, feel. This is really common in metal. It's also used by rock bands from time to time, but they move in and out of it, whereas it will run throughout the duration of many metal songs.

This type of feel is often used with power chords and a pedal tone. It has that sense of urgency, pushing ahead of the beat.

 **FEEL 2 - 2:05**

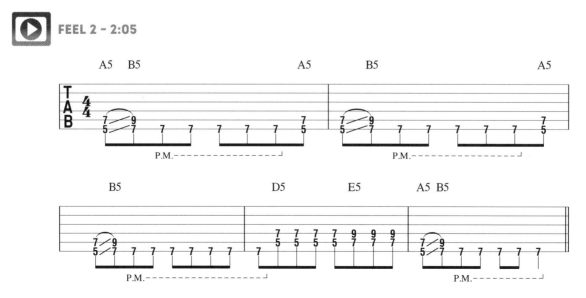

DRAGGED FEEL

Let's pedal that open A string again, but this time, let's attack the string slightly *behind* the drums.

FEEL 3 - 2:20

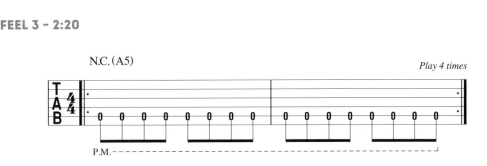

As you can hear, this time I let the drums lead as opposed to me leading them, which is what I did in the first example. The first feel is sort of a marching feel; it's very regimented and rigid. The second feel is a more relaxed or "dragged" feel. I learned the latter by listening to Jimmy Page and John Bonham. It's just a really relaxed, backbeat thing. It's so subtle that, if I hadn't explained it to you, you might not have even picked up on it. But, if you go back and listen to it again, the first feel sounds very tight and stiff, and the second one feels like it sashays or swings a little bit. It's all due to the fact that one beat is coming after the other, which gives it a walking feel.

SWING FEEL

This example's feel is a little more deliberate than the previous two:

FEEL 4 - 3:53

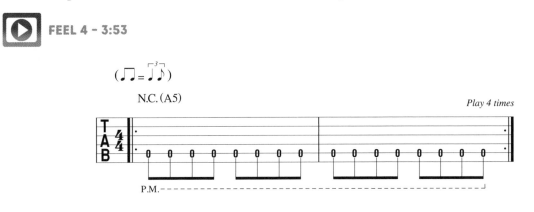

It's called *swing feel*. If you've heard boogie-woogie rock 'n' roll like this…

FEEL 5 - 4:25

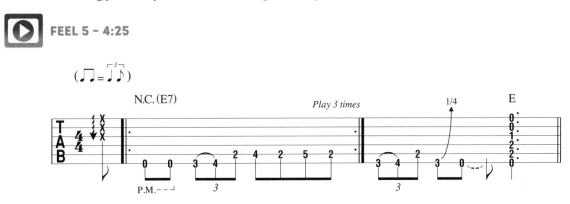

…then you've heard swing feel (also called "shuffle feel").

Here's another example using swing feel:

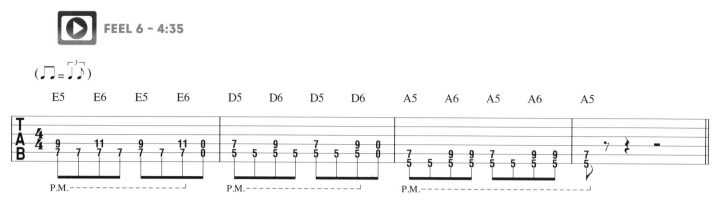

FEEL 6 - 4:35

Swing feel is based on a triplet feel and is really effective. You should learn the differences between pushing, pulling, and swinging the beat. These feels are essential to playing rock 'n' roll rhythm guitar.

Here's one last example incorporating swing feel:

FEEL 7 - 5:00

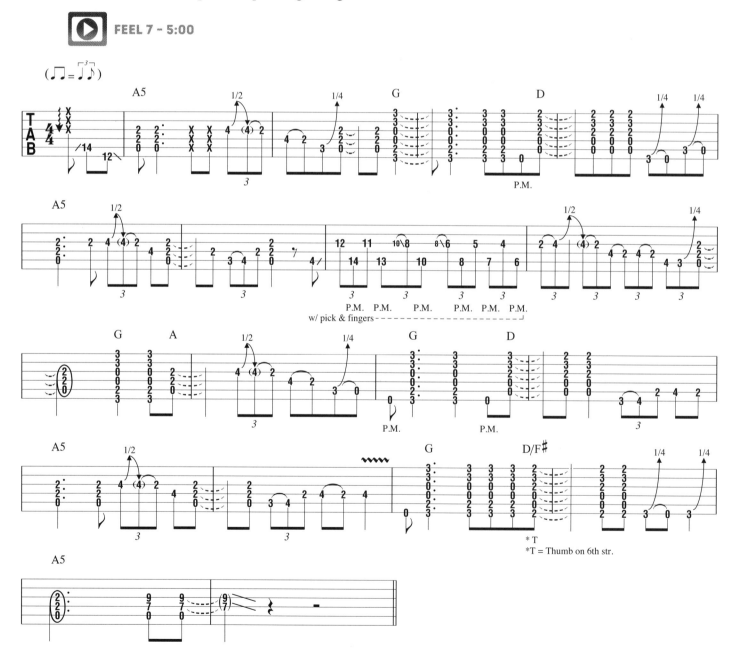

Remember: if you're not moving your body—and you're just thinking about it—then you're never going to connect with the music. You've got to feel it in your body!

CHAPTER 11
ALTERNATE TUNINGS

DROP D TUNING

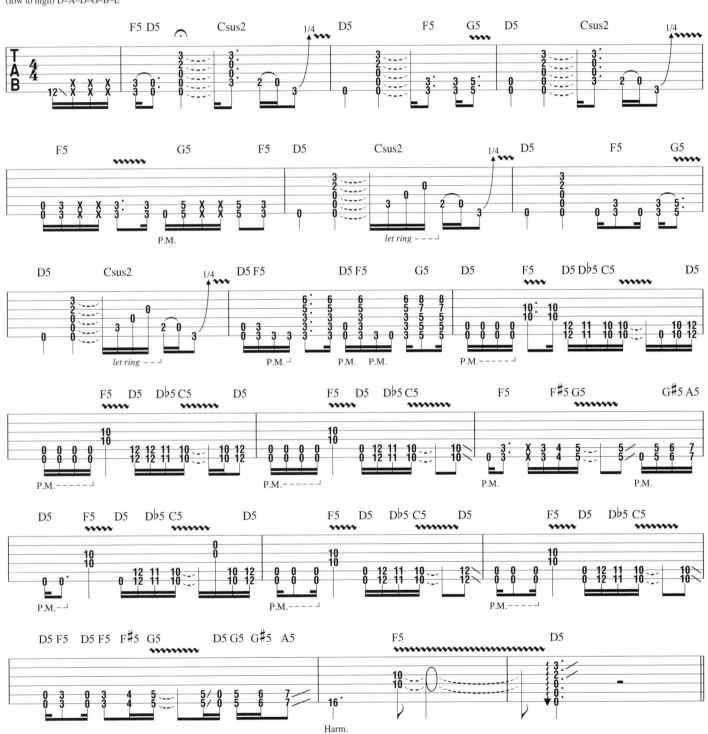

In this chapter, I want to talk to you about *open tunings*. Open tunings are guitar tunings other than standard that create a chord when all six open strings are played. They open a whole new door to walk through with your music. This first one, drop D, is not necessarily an open tuning, but it is an *alternate* tuning. It's simply standard tuning with the low E string detuned a whole step to D: D–A–D–G–B–E.

Drop D tuning allows you to play the 4ths shape on the bottom two strings, although this interval is actually a 5th due to the new tuning. The reason so many rock guitar players love this tuning is because you can move through your chord changes so quickly. Check out the example below.

 TUNINGS 2 - 1:53

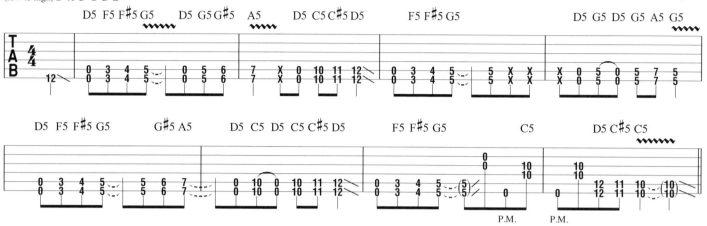

You can get some unbelievably cool stuff with this tuning:

 TUNINGS 3 - 2:09

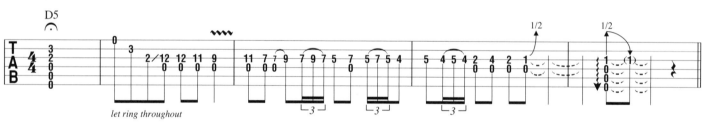

With this tuning, you can also use the upper and lower D strings in conjunction with one another:

 **TUNINGS 4 - 2:31**

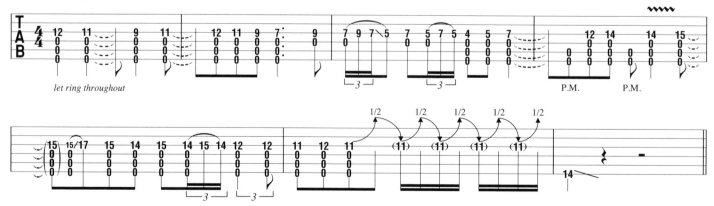

It's a great tuning. You'll use it a lot.

OPEN G TUNING

Now here's an example in open G tuning (D–G–D–G–B–D):

 TUNINGS 5 - 2:48

Open G tuning:
(low to high) D–G–D–G–B–D

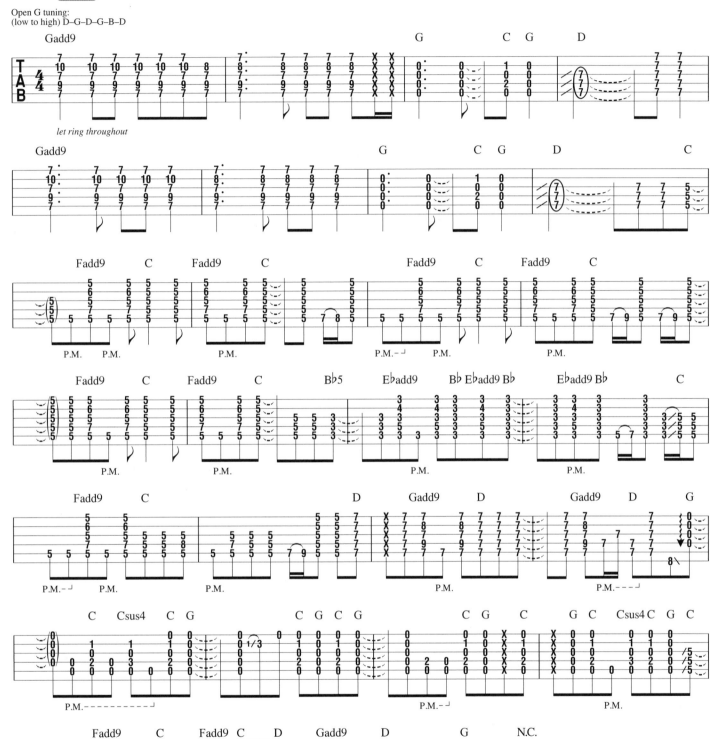

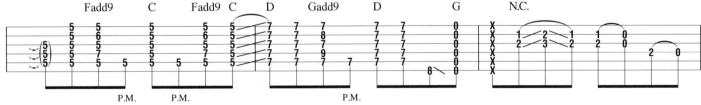

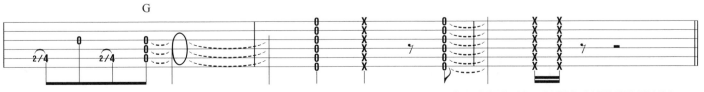

I love this tuning—it's one of my favorites. Although not my forte, this tuning is wonderful for slide playing. Open G is a well-known tuning used by players such as Keith Richards, Ronnie Wood, and the guys from the Black Crowes, among others.

Here's another example in open G tuning:

 TUNINGS 6 - 4:22

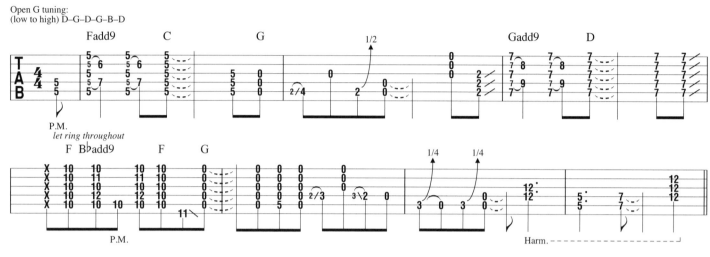

Open G is really inspirational and fun to play around with. It's best to just experiment with different voicings, like this:

 **TUNINGS 7 - 5:19**

Open G... you'll have a lot of fun with this one!

DADGAD TUNING

Our last alternate tuning is DADGAD. The tuning's name and pronunciation ("dad-gad") come from the order of the pitches of the strings, low to high: D–A–D–G–A–D.

 TUNINGS 8 - 5:55

DADGAD tuning:
(low to high) D–A–D–G–A–D

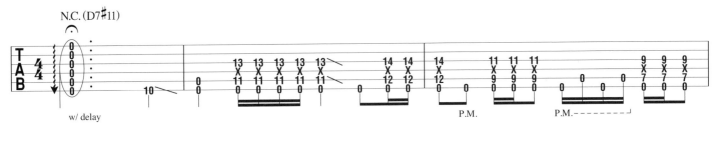

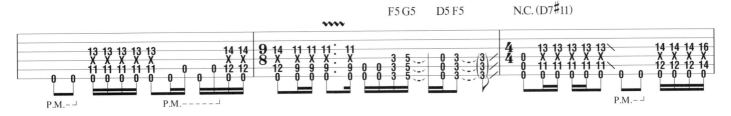

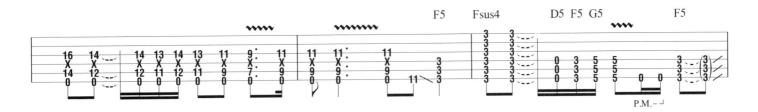

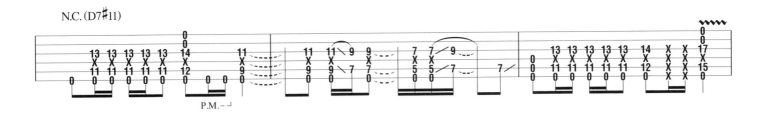

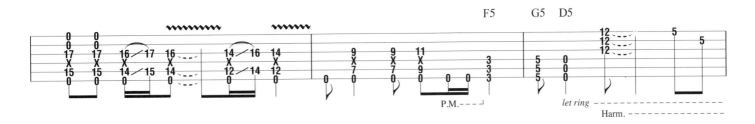

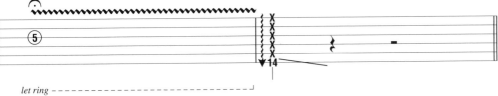

I really like this tuning. It is used extensively by Jimmy Page, and a lot of slide players use it as well. Many great voicings can come from this tuning when combined with moves that you can do with just one finger:

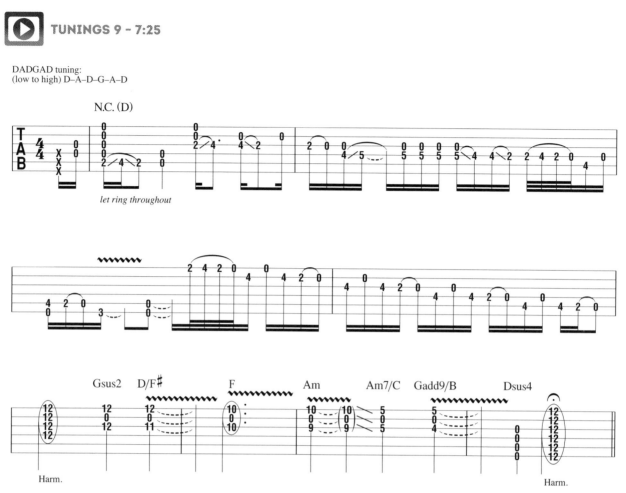

TUNINGS 9 - 7:25

Just get into the tuning and experiment. Before long, you'll find your own cool stuff.

CHAPTER 12
GETTING GREAT RHYTHM TONE AND USING EFFECTS

▶ TONE 1 - 0:00

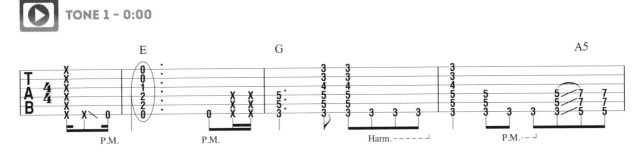

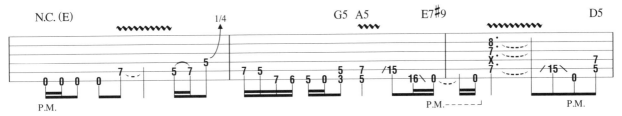

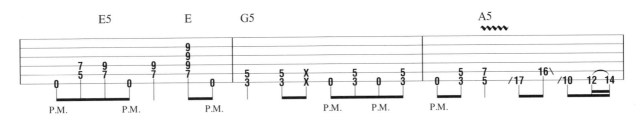

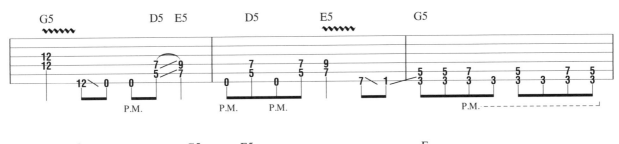

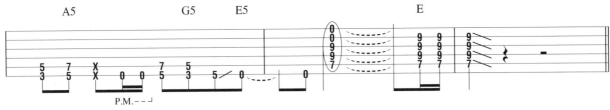

In this last chapter, I want to talk about a very important part of your playing: your tone. First and foremost, tone really does come from your hands. That said, you do need a great guitar and amp. If 20 different guys pick up the same guitar, each one will sound totally different. Therefore, don't think that you need $50,000 worth of equipment; you just need a good sounding amp and guitar as a starting point. They will inspire you to improve your chops and refine your guitar playing. If you find yourself fighting your instrument, you're probably not going to put in the time you need to get where you want to be as a player, or you'll just step away from it altogether. Try to get yourself a good, well-built, brand-name guitar and a good, solid, reliable amplifier with speakers that sound good.

THE GUITAR

The first thing I want to talk about is the guitar. In the video, I'm playing a Gibson Les Paul. I take good care of it because a guitar needs to be maintained. Guitars get played and bumped around and, even though they're made out of wood, sometimes they forget they're not trees anymore. At the end of the guitar neck is a *truss rod*. Some guitars have it exposed where the neck bolts to the body, while others offer access to the truss rod from the headstock. The truss rod allows you to straighten the guitar's neck, which will start to curve due to moisture (or lack thereof) in the air. The winter months typically have less moisture in the air, whereas summer months are humid.

The frets and fretboard need to be cleaned and you need to keep your guitar's *intonation* adjusted, which is something that should be done by a trained technician or luthier if you're not accustomed to doing it yourself. Adjusting the intonation is done at the bridge of the guitar.

It's also important to have good tone and volume *potentiometers*, or "pots," on your guitar—pots that don't crackle and pop. They, too, need to be cleaned from time to time. Good pickups and pickup selectors are also important. You can buy some really nice, inexpensive guitars today, but sometimes the problem with those guitars is the cheap electronics that are placed in them, including cheap pickups, which compromise the instrument. If you put some decent, affordable pickups and pots in your guitar, for just $200, you could have an outstanding guitar. You don't need to spend $5,000.

THE AMPLIFIER

Now let's talk about the amplifier. I'm an aficionado of *tube amplifiers*. There are a million brands out there, and I've pretty much tried them all, and what I would recommend is finding yourself a great-sounding tube amp. It will give you the authentic rock texture that you're probably looking for.

With respect to rhythm guitar playing, I always tell people that you want to stay away from tons and tons of distortion. The distortion I'm playing with in the video is still pretty clear, but it's about as distorted as I'd want to get—period. The more distortion you add to the sound of your guitar, the smaller it sounds and the farther away it gets from the listener. I know it's fun and easy to play with a lot of distortion, but it's important that all of the work that you're putting into your guitar playing comes across to people so they can enjoy it. Therefore, lean towards a cleaner sound. You can use your volume control to roll back some of the distortion, adjusting it to fit the song or part that you're playing, keeping in mind that the cleaner the tone, the better it cuts through.

You'll also get different textures from your pickups. Learn to use them separately and in conjunction with one another. By experimenting with different positions of your volume control(s) and different pickup combinations, you're going to get all kinds of nice textures.

EFFECTS

Effects are the frosting on your tone cake. I like to use effects tastefully. Too many effects can be a disaster when playing with a band or recording music. Like distortion, when you start to add too many effects, your tone starts to disappear.

Start with a nice, chunky rhythm sound that has depth. Next, try adding some *delay*—say, 400–600 milliseconds. It adds a nice little texture to your playing. You can also try some *reverb*. Again, don't go crazy with it, especially with dirty guitar tones. Reverb is wonderful for certain clean sounds, but too much reverb on a distorted tone is not a good combination, as your guitar sound will disappear.

It's always good to have something driving your guitar sound a little bit. If you have an amp that you can set to where your tone starts to break up—it has an edge to it but you can clean it up with your volume knob—a *fuzz* or *overdrive* pedal can give your sound a boost. In the video, I have a fuzz pedal. What I like about fuzz pedals with respect to rhythm playing is that most of them have a tendency to clean up very nicely, even though they're boosting and distorting the signal.

Modulation (chorus, phaser, flanger, etc.) is another effect that I like to use. In the video, I'm using an effect similar to a Uni-Vibe, which is a rotary effect. My main point is that using a few effects sparingly can be really inspirational and add a nice touch to what you're trying to convey when you're playing rhythm guitar.

CLOSING JAM

Before we wrap things up, I want to offer a few suggestions that will help you develop your rhythm playing more quickly and efficiently.

1. Practice your rhythm playing with a drum machine, looper, or metronome. While the latter is not as fun or inspirational to practice with as the others, it'll still help you improve your timing.

2. Listen to other guitarists, preferably great ones. Listen to their tones, riffs, timing, and feel. Pay close attention to the way they lock in with the drums and bass.

3. Great rhythm players also understand the importance of space. Try to incorporate space into your own playing to make it more powerful.

It's important to know that great rhythm playing makes for great-feeling music. Good luck and keep on jammin'!

▶ CLOSING JAM - 0:42

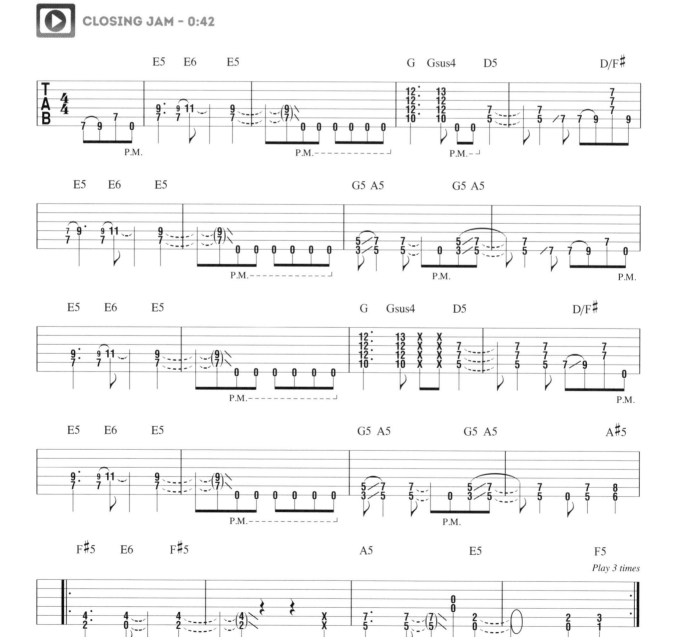

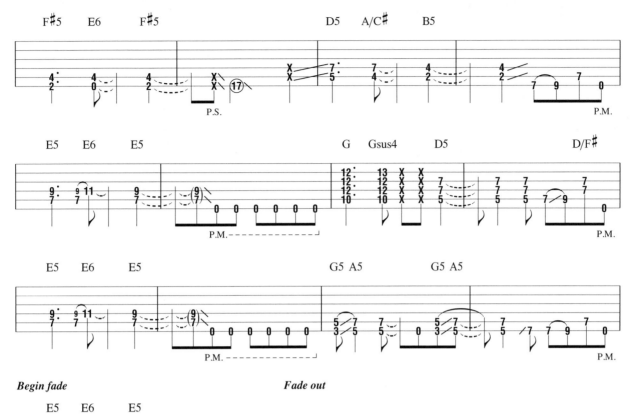

Begin fade

Fade out

Get Better at Guitar

...with these Great Guitar Instruction Books from Hal Leonard!

101 GUITAR TIPS
INCLUDES TAB

STUFF ALL THE PROS KNOW AND USE

by Adam St. James

This book contains invaluable guidance on everything from scales and music theory to truss rod adjustments, proper recording studio set-ups, and much more. The book also features snippets of advice from some of the most celebrated guitarists and producers in the music business, including B.B. King, Steve Vai, Joe Satriani, Warren Haynes, Laurence Juber, Pete Anderson, Tom Dowd and others, culled from the author's hundreds of interviews.

00695737 Book/Online Audio $16.99

AMAZING PHRASING
INCLUDES TAB

50 WAYS TO IMPROVE YOUR IMPROVISATIONAL SKILLS

by Tom Kolb

This book/CD pack explores all the main components necessary for crafting well-balanced rhythmic and melodic phrases. It also explains how these phrases are put together to form cohesive solos. Many styles are covered – rock, blues, jazz, fusion, country, Latin, funk and more – and all of the concepts are backed up with musical examples. The companion CD contains 89 demos for listening, and most tracks feature full-band backing.

00695583 Book/CD Pack.................................$19.95

BLUES YOU CAN USE – 2ND EDITION

by John Ganapes

This comprehensive source for learning blues guitar is designed to develop both your lead and rhythm playing. Includes: 21 complete solos • blues chords, progressions and riffs • turnarounds • movable scales and soloing techniques • string bending • utilizing the entire fingerboard • and more. This second edition now includes audio and video access online!

00142420 Book/Online Media.................................$19.99

FRETBOARD MASTERY
INCLUDES TAB

by Troy Stetina

Untangle the mysterious regions of the guitar fretboard and unlock your potential. *Fretboard Mastery* familiarizes you with all the shapes you need to know by applying them in real musical examples, thereby reinforcing and reaffirming your newfound knowledge. The result is a much higher level of comprehension and retention.

00695331 Book/Online Audio $19.99

FRETBOARD ROADMAPS – 2ND EDITION

ESSENTIAL GUITAR PATTERNS THAT ALL THE PROS KNOW AND USE

by Fred Sokolow

The updated edition of this bestseller features more songs, updated lessons, and a full audio CD! Learn to play lead and rhythm anywhere on the fretboard, in any key; play a variety of lead guitar styles; play chords and progressions anywhere on the fretboard; expand your chord vocabulary; and learn to think musically – the way the pros do.

00695941 Book/CD Pack.................................$14.95

GUITAR AEROBICS
INCLUDES TAB

A 52-WEEK, ONE-LICK-PER-DAY WORKOUT PROGRAM FOR DEVELOPING, IMPROVING & MAINTAINING GUITAR TECHNIQUE

by Troy Nelson

From the former editor of *Guitar One* magazine, here is a daily dose of vitamins to keep your chops fine tuned! Musical styles include rock, blues, jazz, metal, country, and funk. Techniques taught include alternate picking, arpeggios, sweep picking, string skipping, legato, string bending, and rhythm guitar. These exercises will increase speed, and improve dexterity and pick- and fret-hand accuracy. The accompanying audio includes all 365 workout licks plus play-along grooves in every style at eight different metronome settings.

00695946 Book/Online Audio $19.99

GUITAR CLUES
INCLUDES TAB

OPERATION PENTATONIC

by Greg Koch

Join renowned guitar master Greg Koch as he clues you in to a wide variety of fun and valuable pentatonic scale applications. Whether you're new to improvising or have been doing it for a while, this book/CD pack will provide loads of delicious licks and tricks that you can use right away, from volume swells and chicken pickin' to intervallic and chordal ideas. The CD includes 65 demo and play-along tracks.

00695827 Book/CD Pack.................................$19.95

INTRODUCTION TO GUITAR TONE & EFFECTS

by David M. Brewster

This book/CD pack teaches the basics of guitar tones and effects, with audio examples on CD. Readers will learn about: overdrive, distortion and fuzz • using equalizers • modulation effects • reverb and delay • multi-effect processors • and more.

00695766 Book/CD Pack.................................$14.99

PICTURE CHORD ENCYCLOPEDIA

This comprehensive guitar chord resource for all playing styles and levels features five voicings of 44 chord qualities for all twelve keys – 2,640 chords in all! For each, there is a clearly illustrated chord frame, as well as *an actual photo* of the chord being played! Includes info on basic fingering principles, open chords and barre chords, partial chords and broken-set forms, and more.

00695224.................................$19.95

SCALE CHORD RELATIONSHIPS
INCLUDES TAB

by Michael Mueller & Jeff Schroedl

This book teaches players how to determine which scales to play with which chords, so guitarists will never have to fear chord changes again! This book/audio pack explains how to: recognize keys • analyze chord progressions • use the modes • play over nondiatonic harmony • use harmonic and melodic minor scales • use symmetrical scales such as chromatic, whole-tone and diminished scales • incorporate exotic scales such as Hungarian major and Gypsy minor • and much more!

00695563 Book/Online Audio $14.99

SPEED MECHANICS FOR LEAD GUITAR
INCLUDES TAB

Take your playing to the stratosphere with the most advanced lead book by this proven heavy metal author. *Speed Mechanics* is the ultimate technique book for developing the kind of speed and precision in today's explosive playing styles. Learn the fastest ways to achieve speed and control, secrets to make your practice time really count, and how to open your ears and make your musical ideas more solid and tangible. Packed with over 200 vicious exercises including Troy's scorching version of "Flight of the Bumblebee." Music and examples demonstrated on CD. 89-minute audio.

00699323 Book/CD Pack.................................$19.95

TOTAL ROCK GUITAR
INCLUDES TAB

A COMPLETE GUIDE TO LEARNING ROCK GUITAR

by Troy Stetina

This unique and comprehensive source for learning rock guitar is designed to develop both lead and rhythm playing. It covers: getting a tone that rocks • open chords, power chords and barre chords • riffs, scales and licks • string bending, strumming, palm muting, harmonics and alternate picking • all rock styles • and much more. The examples are in standard notation with chord grids and tab, and the audio includes full-band backing for all 22 songs.

00695246 Book/Online Audio $19.99